D1600289

UGLY DUCKLING PRESSE

One Sleeps the Other Doesn't
© 2011 Jacqueline Waters

ISBN: 978-1-933254-83-8

Cataloging-in-publication data is available from the Library of Congress.

Distributed to the trade by
Small Press Distribution
www.spdbooks.org

Available directly from UDP and through our partner bookstores:
www.uglyducklingpresse.org/orders
www.uglyducklingpresse.org/bookstores

This book is funded in part by a grant
from the New York State Council on the Arts.

First Edition 2011
Printed in the USA

Ugly Duckling Presse
The Old American Can Factory
232 Third Street #E-002
Brooklyn, NY 11215

www.uglyducklingpresse.org

ONE SLEEPS THE OTHER DOESN'T

Jacqueline Waters

ONE SLEEPS THE OTHER DOESN'T

A PLOY

                    a plugged-in glow globe throwing
                    thumbprints of land, islets of the outer Pacific
                    over snow
                    stuffing up gaps
                    in the hospital hot/cool unit.

no sleep at first, dream
about a patch of bog
paved over by the broad margin
Thoreau loves to his life:

"I love a broad margin to my life"
                              —Thoreau.

                    it was lovely to say
                              that *it* was raining
                              and to mean
                                        that *part of you* was low: half the pleasure
                                        was suspecting yourself
                                        on to something, the rest

                              fell from following
                              the first pleasure's lead:
                              opening a book on the bar
                              in front of each empty chair
                              setting yourself
                              at the bar's far end
                              till night, your own cloud of it
                              ran right to the orbs of your eyes.

                    no emotion is pleasing!
                    each must be rejected
                    replaced by an opposite

in turn rejected and replaced by yet another
strain of undifferentiated sentiment

till longing collapses
into repair
and the silvered edges
 ebb themselves equal, eager
 to stand there elapsed
 by the great airy lapses
 you find in your way
 until you find your way
or till you find your ways
have rearranged you slightly
 as a margin rearranges slightly
 what has mostly been lived
 by sight.

Phil-

As a movie it asks

we look at a grave

read a headstone, notice a man

tending to the overturned earth

atop an adjacent plot

.

                    not

calculate the tightness of the shot

ask if the filmer had a permit, or if Woodstock, Illinois

was used again

as a stand-in for Punxsutawney: later cold is told

by close-up:

picnic plate

eking out icicles, dump trucks "doing double duty"

as plows

prodding last night's mix

under orange nets for precaution

and *if* the task of every spiritual act

is to return the debate

to some knowable place in the self: a center ring,

  if the circus is your go-to thing, or a center square

  if you like towns

with four-stop-sign intersections

  and a vehicle to hesitate in

  long enough

to torment three other drivers—

  and *if* the bells will ring

  all through the county

  when the groundhog responds to a tap

at the door of his stump-shaped cage

      though he won't *respond*, rather agree

  not to die

  before the handlers of the Inner Circle

  can lift him by his middle

  and dangle his forelegs

      in a cynical show of force—

  Phil, Phil, Phil repeats the crowd, frenzied as a frenzied crowd

and *if* we wish to stay in touch

with our *best* impressions,

those we can scan,

    approve of,

        put on

        as a teen selects a record

        getting the group up

        to rock around the record

    then we will have to look into *our ignorance,*

    though access grow patchy

    and the view

    an x-ing out of gulls

    calm as bags of weeds

    broken open over a teen—

for *if you feel*, who cannot feel, some doubt

    then *you must execute*, who cannot do, some cure:

    if these assorted ifs

    be easily pushed

into a freezable pile

then you must take great pains

from those who no longer deserve

formal feeling:

you must reason with creeps who crushed mills

who grew from mills' good looms

long-playing brocade dresses—

and you must stay close by, where "close by" equals "shouting distance"

where scheduled to happen is "slated to occur"

where when you say "slated"

you reveal your consumption of journalism

and a suspicion your insides

are important enough

to be journalized about

minus response

to repeated requests for comment:

regarding comment

you remain unrequited,

will not grab your half

of that moth-eaten cloth,

nor imagine it was ever

eaten by moths—for to acquire new clichés

would demand new wars

and new people to staff them,

and the *poverty* of your greed

is unlike any other:

from great distance

objects come

hold up their secondary merit

to your primary gaze

drop on you the leisure

of moments of suffering, proffering lemon

eau-de-cologne,

tying sweet grass

in striped cotton suiting

eating the choices out

from porch to lawn,

lawn to tip

of barbecue tool,

tool to mouth,

sleep—

while *over frost-crusted fields*

and down

descends the crowd

from Gobbler's Knob, warned of winter

while still within it—

and it *seems like a pain*

to be so self-conscious: to dread the weather

you are already weathering

your silhouette transferred

to soft-paste porcelain: translucent

as a bluebird's wing

through forty-five minutes' drive

from a pile of arhar lentils

where an eroded strip of asphalt

becomes a dusty, unpaved lane

to the uneasy churches

of Western Pennsylvania

whether newly lifted or

poorly attended, whether smeared with an adverb

or *two*, whether

volunteer divers

    scrub the sea lion famous

    for making paintings on acrylic panels

    while zoo PR

    hints the magic 1,000,000th visitor number

    will hit:

and if Homer's feasting scenes

include talk turned in

by heroes attending the feast

as themself

while representing

someone else

so as the groundhog named Phil my first symptom

is pain

from impinged-upon

pain management system: synapses then vacuum up sensation

and post it to the plane below the plane

I'm pleading to stay still upon, though it be struck by others

though it explode

into large-angled asteroids, whose life

will be long, drifting off

as small-angled, medium-angled

space rocks

dropped on the people

pushed out of an area

who followed you for miles

hurling objects

they'd picked up from the ground

wishing for a word

to dump like water

on the dirty looks they received: we came to the atrium

of a large apartment building, its hexagonal walls

    papered over with papers

    in the shapes of undersea weeds: not that nearness to the sea

    beautifies anything: ships empty their latrines, clean their holds

    and a hard yellow foam

        forms a 1-pixel stroke on the coast: some odors we recognize

        only when our noses

brush up against what smells—to have it, not give it, take a long time

faking it in inventory

and finally crush it

is just another *way*. Nor is this not *not* a cliché: I'm not appalled

    I'm afraid

    of getting appalled

    and revealing myself

    appallable: maybe you'll visit Punxsutawney

by Groundhog Day

and bring forth one

singular sensation: the final query

at the end of a string of queries: *what is the meaning of this?*

a Nigerian priest

just used it on TV, having returned to his parish

to find his church boarded up

by arrogant parishioners, the last of them

rapping at the door with a rake's tines: *what*

is the meaning of this? I included the phrase

  in a draft once

  and it was struck from the draft by a friend, not struck

by the friend, but struck by his advice,

the word "weak" written

in the right margin, and so the phrase, like the priest,

was stricken. "What happened"

  is what we usually say, what has passed,

  why are we out of the cage of our comfortable chair,

  why by chair do I mean *understanding*

and by cage, *conceit*—conceit to call it a *cascade*

the waterfall rounding out the town

that runs into a pond

that feeds a stream running into another

more skeptical pond: *what*

(the break provides the accentual pause)

is the meaning of this?

khaki-clad constable

positioned by the brick kiln

hefts rifle to shoulder, aims with room to maneuver,

works the bolt action

over dummy bullets and a cartridge case

anticipating

tourist incursion, or another

wintry week, another turn

of the cheek to receive

the haymaker: and thus things change

even the "things you cannot change"

that surplus powering the acrobat

swinging across the stage, holding herself nearly horizontal

as her hair blows in a breeze

her head created—

      or killers drive up, shoot, pick up your body like a sack

      and burn it in the outskirts

      of Casavatore: every refusal, in other words,

      provokes another blow: every bond, be it

      affection, ownership, religion

      is a concession

         to the competition:

how often "pain" has saved you

from certain disaster, or more often the disaster

of a pile of certainty: *as in The Odd Couple*

when Jack Lemmon seals an envelope

marked "To My Wife and Beloved Children"

moves to the window

      ready to jump

from the ninth floor

of the Hotel Flanders

driven to the end of the line

by pain occurring

pre-movie,

       pre-plot: *but Jack Lemmon*

is foiled by a stuck window: presses one way

       windmills his arms to switch his grip

       presses again

       till his eyes widen

both hands fly to his back: *Oh no.*

Plan thwarted

by *painful* back pain

Jack Lemmon staggers to the bed

and reclines: cut to Lemmon

       exiting the hotel

down to the drugstore for a cure

—but having *thought through* the act

having set a baseline

to communicate doubt, hesitancy, confidence

and resolve: having gotten a monitor

about twelve inches high

and considered its face your mirror: so that whenever you feel strong emotion

of *any* kind, or wish to scratch your eye, rub your nose, move a toothpick

    around in your mouth,

    tap the table with your fingertips, you go out and drive a car

    and know you know

how what you're *feeling* looks: though trees, boulders, telephone poles

    seem to fall from every direction, one after another

    as you move down the street: a ball bounces in

chased by an obstacle

shorter than the foreshortened

hood of your car: and old people foil you, as do toddlers,

perambulators, ambulances, fruit wagons, bicycles and a sawhorse

around a pothole big as a right front wheel.

    Or you find a tutor, thus turning the ball over to the other team which scores even more and widens its lead—

your next stop

will be a moment-by-moment second-guessing

"am I hot" "am I cold"

till a path is formed

by your constant aboveground treading

and when showing it to your neighbor at the table

you think about shaking your head

at the difficulty she has

sitting up in her chair: some equation must be at work

some principle whereby weak units, fragile when combined

grow stronger when *separated*

and you start to think about this

as if you are *Time* magazine, aiming to focus on one thing

and make it stand for every thing

ruined by the huge currents

that wrap winds around the world

thinking the point of thinking

was to establish new, though false, content for your day

then chronicle the unraveling

of the content you came out here with

—in hunters' camouflages

fastened by a single zipper

stretching from pelvis to neck

nature compels us to be wicked

but the town elders ensure we're good.

We have thus far

described a holiday

in the American state

of Pennsylvania

but haven't described it,

have stolen from it a set of stills,

singling them out of the emergence

of good from likely to lead

to a reminder that *you* and *I*

stayed up all night in an aisle at Rite Aid

to *make it to the Knob by five*

—and *if* I aim to examine

wreckage aggressively sought

by treasure hunters, place it alongside treasure

wrecked by speakers

whose explanations have triggered

the evaporation of value

from one's *observed beloved*, convincing the sun

to rise and set over a world

less conducive

to *normal* reverie

—if I'm still worried the Inner Circle

eats Punxsutawney Phil

each August at the Groundhog barbecue,

stag, with roasted corn and homemade lager

then I don't hope to atone nor regain

an event I attended, a place I was

for a moment: my day, its night

hot and cold tap handles

rotated in quick succession

and the water passed from hand to hand

amid ten thousand ski jackets

palling around on Mahoning Street: around the ice carving contest's

surviving detritus, around the local band tented

to entertain teens—

and if you misplaced your keys

ten years ago, or dropped an aquarium tank

mid-fill, the look on your face

was essentially the same

it would be

if those things happened *now*: your reactions

as announced by your expressions

don't change: face

makes its choices until choice

ceases: and thereafter, *actions* are key:

your hesitation

like a very nice hotel, is the gap in the mirror hung in the trellis meant to

siphon off the foliage

and show more flowers, doubled white asters

over geranium-patterned plaster—*doubt*

comes into French poetry when Apollinaire in "Zone"

writes of the little street

of which he's forgotten the name

"dont j'ai oublié le nom"

not doubt, of course, more like

freedom to err, as in conversation

so long as the error

expresses the skepticism

of which doubt is an unfortunate *symptom*:

—but *this* symptom is a madness: let it pass

regard it as a lowly opponent

assigned by bracket

at your luxury tennis club: greet it

from behind the waist-high net

as though you know

two trench-digging robotic arms

will open a moat around the road

that takes the city in: it's not a city, seen from beneath

or owned from above—

        or three or four men

        crushed the mill, which was itself a kind of crusher

for the rich, who wouldn't have to eat money

if the poor didn't have to generate

grippers for tying sutures, clot-busting drugs,

objects that stop

at their own edges

then attach like a magnet to the next

      shipment of boxed objects—

encouraged to hope, impassioned by doubt,

you should like to explain why you

      might have built the mills then crushed the mills,

      from one finger expelled the flames

that lit the American rustbelt

and reduced it to its fields

that all that move in them

could be yours:

    water falling

off the skate of Osgood and disappearing behind the net: a charge of *icing*

will end the Penguins' third: suspect your lapses

of *behooving* you:

of being leaps

over important turns in the path: we are almost walking

over crooked hills

pulled together with broad thick bands

their barren tops

crumpling to receive

giant prints of our foot:

late winter afternoon plus sun

plus cars on shopping trips

plus *Free HBO, no pool*

Continental breakfast, complimentary wireless, no pool

Pool, no HBO, Showtime but you have to pay for it

What is the mood called

where you want to kill everyone else's enthusiasm

and figure out that you can

Guard of an Eaten Collage: A Guard: I

It is night. In the embracing happy man
Just released from ninja fights
Along a fallen tree
Over a madman's gorge
A short chop at the air
With the edge of the affected hand
Places the chops like flowers
Evenly along a central stem

Funny charwoman
It's a nice night
I could be wrong
You hear people say all kinds of shit
Like I wouldn't lean my back on that it's sticky
Or did I ever tell you
That thing you strive for
With everyone watching
Might have been yours
As you lifted a foot
And composed an aside
You almost said, or forgot in thought
Or harbored with everyone knowing?

All night, at all hours, the screech of the squall swept down

I saw it wholly in me
Then in it I saw myself quite apart from myself
And with its royal movements
It poured itself entirely toward me
Again I saw all over it
The motions of others were stirring
I heard their songs
Which they whispered at their descent

Charwoman you're in the day
You put one hand up to glisten
God looks down
To see humankind
And I sink a fist in the side of your neck

I've got a lot of shit to contend with
People call me they say things like
I'm just calling to see if you have anything

The man heard noise
And started his crawl
Along the enemy parapet

You act like I'm being a fragile egg but fuck it ha ha
I sit here a month at a time it's not wrong
Especially, but a sequence of grace
Asks for movement from or to: the window washers
Of the Verizon building
Start out at the top
Are lowered at a ratio
Of wash to lower
Till the end of the day
Finds them dead

Go drench a couch with your weeping
I am like one who does not hear
Turn now be gracious to me
I took you out of a net
By you I will crush a troop
And walk upon a broad place
With a right hand pleasuring me

Dear man and/or lady:
Behold, I am against you

I am ingots of lead on the eyelids and lead in the head à la grande manière
I am one eyeball took place without telling the other
Which place it could take
Out of the way of all the eyeballs. I was born
Politely, then notified the hand
Cultivating in the narrow spaces between trees
That said I'll pull your eyes out
If they would come out

The man itched to look back
Broke the heads of dragons in waters
Grappled and fell in the gutter

Dear man and/or lady:

The question might be put this way:
To some, the world has disclosed itself as too vast; there is nothing left
For them to do
But shut their eyes
And disappear. To others, on the contrary, the world is too didactic, a
Series of inward measurings-up
Revealed as too beautiful
Too bold in the way
Of the head beneath the sky

You enter, you go Hi, I go
Hello. You go onward and I go next time you swipe your I.D. or I stop fucking you

Acorns on a pick come
If I were hungry I wouldn't tell
I would put it to flight
I would aim at its faces with blows

Boughs grow out of you woman
As though you were a kneeling leg

And yet I take your head
And line it up with a floor plank edge

The man subtracted an ice
From his own built drink
The man hurled his cuff
At the other man's cuff

People come by
Who'd like to take a fork
And stab you in the balls
And I am here
To give you hope
While that's happening

The Garden of Eden a College

I.

In the initial guess
land foamed over the plain
dust came up
waist-high between the buildings
where a puppet lolled
in uncoordinated rigging

       Whatever way the day began
it's hot out now. Oh mental widows
after weeks of pith helmets and ground meal
having a whole conversation without the word now
now you I recognize
not by sight, you red jake
but by your exaggerated feel
    for the bridge, the sun, the hedge
    behind me where I hear some rising
    and some falling

*

I hold my own, at cross-purposes
to the game, creeping over a hillock
eliding first defenses
Custer whose season
abhorred scum or its sensations
is so-so as a magical interest
At night I want not to sleep
in the morning more so
Whatever was it
caused me to think my life *specific*
dropped into a wicker chair
rattling off cocaine
with a feeling of arousal, a sensitivity

to tiny differences, no stronger than
one state of mind passing into another
miming the resolution of my affairs
though my affairs
are just my questions
their proliferation
wrung by a rotted clock
reverence pitted
in little stabs at the held pincushion
What about landscapes perceived by trespassing
do they count in the meaning of the injured mind?
And whoever felt a *single* sensation
unaware of thousands of others
succeeding so rapidly
as to leave one razored impression
frightened of its own perpendicular
to my accumulated groans

*

Lampwick says

      I met you in Freshman Composition
      where the night wind thrashed in every direction
      You waved your hand as a matter of spirit

Room for the *right* person, yes—
I don't have moments I have instants
with ticketed insects
that keep returning
I won't go up I'll feign laundry
lots of saints or no
trying to consider what Lampwick said

      Right left or straight

No, trying to *consider* what Lampwick said

       I am Jackie. You increase my curiosity.

Jackie what do you say to
eagerness, the old flourless
slab of land, calm passages punched

out of the Seaport district:
ready, set, say

I won't smell after this will I

Jackie if only wasting time got rid of it

Lampwick I feel there is a gentility
presupposed by flower shops
parties and prizes
that is unobtainable in our times

Jackie you need the life
scared out of you

Lampwick I fear I haven't much to say
and am unnerved
about who to say it to

Jackie you have some nerve
has no one remembered to hush you
in this particular weather
their interest strung behind, so far
and in nouns so low
as to need *bringing to*?

What's the earth with mosses anyway
a true shade will vault
booting out her lack
proud to serve the uneven surface
with evenhanded soreness
though you seem to suffer
from a turn in the hour
a tendency to imitate the other
in proportion to nearby horseshit
which produces the "avid" look

        Oh margarine in its armored state
the fructification of keeping seeds
starlit in cover, the mumbling especialness
of a dumb tongue. Crucial as a blast
what the dark thunder
tunes in to
during ostracization exercises

I like to get exercise
It keeps me stationed here
in the well-vented walls
and sidling fronds
of Kaneohe

*

In the erection of a human pyramid on waterskis
one can be helped by one's *inner moral*

No you don't know or no you do

I am moving off the soft plow of Enlightenment
darkness rolls in
so easily it is not darkness

I only want there to be repudiation on earth
not scams
or a street behind this one
sharing a humdrum quality
with the unspecific rest of us
for whom there is a saying, saying
        the more you repeat a vow
           the more conversant you are
           with repetition, the curds
        just allowed to assemble, the grass
        just taken out of the ground

        I wish I could repeat after
        you but almost always I'd rather
        the garden were something
it isn't: applied to the ground
in patches, for instance
zoological in its ambition
to cover the whole

*

Lampshade I am under you for a fitting

Do my eyes look OK in this head?

*

Ugly results. Should I go and get a piano
If bringing the knee into *attitude*
and turning can serve the bridges
that don't suffice, that aren't
ready for the washer—
the more you travel toward ability
the farther you are from technical celibacy

and sun collects
living beings of the east
the way bright quick eye movements
piece out the lemon tree
as each lemon
worries its angle of presentation

Yet I would
regain the brain I left
last Christmas
achieving etiquette
with a whiff of regret
I have known myself a niece
late yet leaning in, reactor-faced
as a summer patch
the weeds all reached
and pulled in
stiller than trophies

II.

Go, I'll explain everything via walkie-talkie

Where were you

     Trying to consider what Grand Central Station said

Where were you

     Bent over a paper made important by the scrutiny I gave it

Poem on the endeavor
to emancipate the soul
from daydreams, hello
Thought, which you must seek out again
and consume in opposition
to these small snow-powdered roots
tapped by the hotel guard
     friendly with me
    frivolous with me
sent by a rat to pick the coat
with the feel of being coaxed
to accept an unpleasant ruse…

Maybe I don't know any better, goes the song

     The "aggressive lost"
     mass at the exit
     Tell me about the way you get interrupted
     then uninterrupted. I agree jasmines are
     bouqueted garbage bags of the inability
     to remember love without pretending
     to atheistic faces in the comforter gaps
     but down swirls ever skyward

Persons find in new words and
new combinations the sin
that most easily besets them—
all beauty is felt as command
in the phantasm of double touch
my hand on your right knee
with sealing wax accuracy

*

You can't be turning me on
and off again, goes the song

I attend the passage of morning rage
sedge bending under the weight of birds
        For the present question
        intelligence is approved
        as something static that invents
                the "me" of violence:
                I can grow my hair longer
                but psychologically, what
                can I become?

I was not drunk, goes the song

Speaking to the moldings
in an over-warm room
of what rises in the night
to soften the scaffold
under whatever patience was, sameness of mobilization?
Sunday-morning artlessness?

Going to the floor
with a furtively placed
lei

Coming up to vertical
curiously trusting
something no one needs to know
things in places they are not likely to be
them there ourselves
mounting the hospitality cart
like a sound made
without any twelve things striking

★

Lampwick says

Oh, we parted. I don't know
it's anything to me
       A grand Plunge, a long Elbow
       A Turin-like apron of lymph-flecked gauze

"Hope you're doin' good"

★

But who-

ever

provided
the more
plausible speculation did win, drawing a Mongolian screen
around the dispute—though perhaps that
was in the 1970s, before they stored giraffes
in a diorama of the savannah
tufts of larval grass
sprung up around hindquarters
the surrounding statuary

culled from our civilization
despair of which, while archaeological
passes to a last protrusion:
her left thumb curled below
her right ear

What brings you here

My legs, what else

What about this job makes you want to pounce all over it

After serving three years
I cannot have a complete thought
without moral enthusiasm
revolving in the rear of my mind

Why are you a good candidate

Short fences, low mounds

Would you like a prolonged
stupid accident, a partial death
both in us
and obliged to us

Excuse me I noticed all this merchandise stuffed in my bags

Do you suppose

No. I move from place to place
without supposing

That supposes a road

Right but I'm looking to get away from that

Jacqueline you must keep taking a
part away you can't have sympathy
for any individual part
Pleasing, never ceasing, you
have patrolled yourself
almost peacefully—
you were the feelings
of one person as modified by
the presence of others
creeping from darkened rooms
to snatch the medium
from the pit dug for her feet

You must learn never to wake up empty-handed

But how will I know

★

Children will work
if they think they're in heaven, goes the song

I've been double crossed
or I've been framed
or my soul broke
when I was playing handball
on the back of a rock
where not for lack of love
but its shortcomings
I played alone

Advice it is
to extort from you
gently across an upturned whack
the no-thing that makes us affectable

a shrift of horrible mist
bounding in from the forest
your hourglass eyes
resting on a paint job's
exaggerated clumps. Oligarchy
redeems consciousness, what else?
An accident in the cabbage aisle
around the side of which
we'd be indebted to find *it*
like a gleam in agate

(These are all very good questions but stop
asking them. You are like us
remember? You like us)

Dangerously the rain dried
pressing her biography
open to a parting
curious for its last
pressure-less clasp
the subject exposed
down to his dendrites

Every superfluity *counts*, I mean it
takes away from attention to something—
which is fine for a while

I marched on Rome it
pulled a gun on me the
passage of fluid through an
organ grinder monkey
sometime after Adam
and before the last
employable
human

All hasty and sensitive
we edge closer, using movements
exclusive to persons
prefaced by jackets and scarves
till there is only this circum-
stantial *feeling*
                of evidence
around which we maneuver
                pressing bastards
into the laps of strangers
their pre-adoptions flush
with cakes and fillings
with mental champagnes
so sincere as to be
insatiable

Jacqueline you ought to suspect the tawny jelly
of difference-oriented reasoning
and learn by delving, ear to sound

Where were you

                Avoiding responsibility
                so as to capture the thrill
                of despising something I once loved

Where were you

Nothing to worry about should
a participant state inside himself
goodbye to strange walls
it looks like standards
were voluntary after all
and movies were there
to erase the feeling
of being peeped at so minutely

Over the Astral building
a relishing of drones
You who cannot hear the noise you have not been making
This is the symbol of that, but not securely
Why don't you know
relics are not separable from their care
and say so before every breeze
headed south like an old rendition

III.

My hay fever temporarily passes. I peer again on the theater
now but partially filled
approach the tiger tap its forehead
hate the tiger

Return, my portion of Lampwick
and be the bore you always meant to
more than not long ago!

     Jacqueline the best way to protect the beavers is to **kill them**

Lampwick this is not what you are looking for
or it is and you are totally embarrassed

        Jacqueline why should anyone be sincere?
        To apprehend the motion
        of what will always be refused?
        Regardless of the consequences, externally
        taught? I am not a moron I just hear winds
        and the winds the winds carry and I
        desire them as fragments of constant heat
        report themselves as stars
        close to the shoulder of a building
        closed between a window
        I desire with a desire so fulfilled
        that desire itself seems arbitrary—
        imposed, like a deadline, arbitrarily
        then accepted as the necessary preface
        to a satisfaction so total
        that recuperation
        will have to begin
        right now

*

Desire's a good start, don't you
think

*

The television dwarfs the apartment it is right
I open and close the refrigerator I am left

holding up "an" end
getting it so we can't see the sky
but can identify
what obscures it: yarn, very soft, white
or the erecting of slitting-mills
and sap factories…

Nothing changes at the parallel
because it's fine for a while
        when you feel the spell break
        after days or weeks
        of poring over complications
        with the industry of a mining engineer, and with a voice
        permitted to extrude from unison
        and slap a security guard
        under green grapefruit and manzanita leaves
        because Lampwick meant *it*
        i.e., he didn't mean *nothing*

*

The New York City police
in copters overhead
getting somebody
committing something

come from wonderment
awe about the world around them
about the individual, the animal, the alien
the flamelet, the molecule
the benches I sat on, the foods
I was near

All love space
objects are space
and one does not think of them as space

*

Yet I know they're never going to get up on a *real* platform
whatever open-ended arrangement
circles its arms to a free flotation
here in the merest
assassination of effort
the lie of a glance to the barre
the three-tiered eyebrow raise
is caught putting up a solution
of infinite consequence:

> Whoever calls, call back
> It'll hurt to store
> feel faceless to exhale
> thus in my typhus
> concatenating emotion
> to movement in the cider trees
> each successive balcony
> trundled with a pistol
> pushing off a foot to
> muffle the door—this kidding,
> what of its freakish
> love of all we touch?

*

Vapor that drapes the refrigerator glass
no matter how unmemorable
splits the pauses between purchases
the way the heavens are said to care.
           They don't. You as a Florentine lisp
           something about our effusive goodness
           floundering above a cloud so thin
           it can barely bedim the sun
yet doing *something*, knowing enough
to second-guess mechanical habit
the flimsy streetlight
rebottled to flare
less listlessly, making sense
of an undemanding sort
until the conversation wanes
in sundry waits
by the hounded door
through cards
handed out in scatter patterns

*

Lampwick says

      I feel
peculiar
          I feel
crowded by

I say
      you have to brace yourself
for warm elements
in the human veneer:

You don't need the aggravation
and can make your own socialization
but the maid answered
and it interested people
You were old flames
expert and able to conceal it
with a butler in every doorway
a telephone on the edge
of every bathtub
as in a musical
built up around technicolor legs

Jackie I see

Lampwick I tire

Busts of leafers-through
with raised maces, how close to instinct is the Romantic project? Is it
merely pleasing, the assuaging of space-sharing?

I can see cars on the FDR
better than Linda Napolitano
who floated over the river
on an alien ray
The sky is almost vague enough
for a new flow of
secrets—a secret empiricism
and that which collects it
trees in piazzas
rails along houses with
green seats in them
a flock of kings
outlined in a mirror
which everybody knows I'll explain
eventually

(So we watched, and sent spies, who pretended to be sincere, that they
might take hold of what was said, and put away their hand, and we
perceived this craftiness, and showed no partiality, but withdrew, and
wore our visors, and gathered out our kin, and were
a fool)

Paraphrase

OK I feel optimistic when I hold your hand

So put that

Shut up

You shut up

You shut up you bureaucratic bullying dog
cock

*

Hills are blue, to pick a color

Second, if you happen to be counting
like countless others numbered among the stars
know that any result
must be firm to prejudices, a waiter descending
by uncorrected magic
for man and beast, while their skulls
form the heavenly vault

to have at you, to make you feel you went away, only to come back with

"I do whatever they want I ESTABLISH RAPPORT"

★

and if ever I break off in the middle
it's because you know the end—
No opposite is so strenuous as to obey an original
For that, the principle
of progressive specification: you become
a vertebrate, rather than some sort of invertebrate
a mammal and not another vertebrate
then you become you, and technology
looms from the forest

In treetops overlooking leaf fill
you and I
are said to see eye to eye
) (

★

I lift the microphone to the tiger attack victim

"I sensed the tiger retreat from me even as I was
hauled backward apart from it"

The fruit has figured out the tree
too long

Indifference is limitless

With primps that
aren't really, feet together
then night

Hello Due to Confusion: A Guard: II

(And now you get another picture
of my mind thinking all this
and know the present terrific moment's
important to me both now
and as snapshot put away
for future soothing nostalgia
And this gives *you* hope,
though you're no longer myself,
the quiet person, loyal only
to the view from my eyes)

Horse

Horse, horse, will you be my mother?
I am a horse. I cannot be your mother.

Think
Of the point at which a disturbance
Intersects itself
To show which side it supports: nobleness
Or misfitness: think of a tampered-with
Racehorse assigned
To the usual oval now think
Of a heat-seeking
Ejaculation into
A can of no-name
Asparagus tips

Stop giving me that job

Think of the weather, fallen from
High, no longer able
To develop, how it can
Only sustain those
Left to its

Consequence: can only excite those left
To care

Would you like to hear a poem I found it in the *Post* it's called The Response

"The Response"

Air-defense planes
were scrambled
but pilots did not
know where to go
or what targets
they were
to interrupt

Once a shootdown
order was given it
was not communicated
to the pilots

★

Ascend, sad thoughts, on golden wings
And implore heaven to freeze up its seams
That no bad martyr will ever get in
To strum the harp
Or make prophetic utterance

★

Take your seats and clam up
Ask yourself this as you
Clam: have you
Ever done more than faint
Cry some tears

Holding your face in your hands
With one eye open
Peering between two fingers
To see if anyone sees?
Sees *you*? I haven't known
What will happen
Very long. We have a will, we find it
Thwarted, this creates
Irritation, the origin of which,
Over time, grows mysterious.
Such mystery provokes
Our intelligence, which then provides
Answers, answers *born* (don't forget) of irritation, and we'll pretend,
And say stuff, and try to make friends, but in our heads this leftover
Feeling after profound
Thwartedness

Behold, I am against you

Hey handguns, assault rifles, marijuana and
crack
       with broccoli to chew
I have to kill $1 of time
       Was there in the room
some lie I said
that has come true?

Every time I put my head to sleep
Consciousness, aiming to interpret
The guilty twinge, intercepts either
The consciousness of Conscience or the Residue
Of recollected Taunts, buzzed in twice, through the same
Poorly locked door
Would you like to hear a poem it's called Protecto

"Protecto"

Subjects pick out the light
and proceed to get
habituated to it

People focused on their hands
get better pry times
with the pry-point
of the hammer claw

I like you
When I think of you
But I don't return to you—I don't, that is, *oblige*
To learn if only by experiencing
Dissatisfaction with all that came before
That things illuminate a nice
October evening: here have a little more of it

They themselves become what they behold

You don't see
Them, I see
Them, they are
Hunting me
Down yet I
Must stay on

This is serious this is hoaxes we're not just
Fucking around I mean wake the
Fuck up you filthy ride hogs

Dear man and/or lady, I have tried to guard your poem but now you and
I exchange looks the way normal people exchange money: man and lady,
you and I can't both be guards. If I tell you this in such words as will

make you think, make you live up to your thinking, have I not done well in telling? Early in my career I guarded a pharmacy, a real masterpiece of variety, and it was out of this pilgrim-motive that I developed a formula for manufacturing guards but then

Like a fool
Started individualizing
Each one

Listen to this thing from Irenaeus:

"The days will come when vines will grow every one of which will have ten thousand branches, and on each branch there will be ten thousand twigs and on each twig ten thousand shoots and on each shoot ten thousand clusters will grow and on each cluster ten thousand grapes, and every single grape, when pressed, will yield five and twenty barrels of wine. And when any one of the saints lays hold of a cluster, another cluster shall cry out: I am better, take me."

*

When I'm up in this club
I think about
Shrinking down and running the length of a dart
Shot to the floor of this club

I think about the dumbest thing is to sing
To train a little monkey
To be a little man
With a stamp of the foot
And a shake of the head

When a person needs protection that person might hire a guard, known to one and all as a bodyguard. Persons who are particularly important or fear for their importance might hire more than one guard, exchanging the bodyguard for the security detail.

Hiring more than one guard communicates to consumers of photographs of the person that the person with more than one guard is more valuable than the person with just one guard.

I thought if my productions would not or could not protect me, I could, at the very least, protect my productions. To protect one production I imagined especially vulnerable I produced other productions to act as its guards.

But I only managed to write two guards, two guards did I write, before

Now I'm thinking of an illusion, and for the illusion I'm thinking of, you'll need two chairs. Place one chair behind another, both chairs facing the same direction, as though you were preparing the room for a concert, but a concert with only two attendees, and you have determined those two attendees, whether for reasons of acoustics or reasons of social hierarchy, must not sit beside one another, but in front of and behind.

Perhaps the concert is even in a corridor, or a narrow passageway, too narrow for most concert instruments, too narrow for aisles of passage to the right and left of the chairs, and wide enough only for a singer, a soprano or tenor, or a mouth organ player, or a laptop computer set to play a playlist composed of music you have judged hospitable to the place you now find yourself, if you have invited yourself to the concert, or have decided to enter the corridor first, followed by the laptop, and followed by the chairs, which will no doubt make you feel trapped, a feeling you will want to incorporate into your playlist, if indeed it is not too late.

For this illusion, called the Pinocchio Illusion, the entrant to the illusion sits in the rear chair. Entrant blindfolds herself. The party to the illusion sits in the fore chair. The entrant's left hand reaches around the

the somnambulism overtook me, and in my somnambulism I placed one to the production's left and one to its right. Two guards were necessary because the production had two exits: its beginning and its end.

But neither the guards nor the details I produced about the guards were secure. My production, despite its protection, could be approached from the front or the rear.

Four guards were necessary, but the last two are not produced, owing to reasons of somnambulism.

party's face and strokes the party's nose. Meanwhile, the entrant's right hand reaches to the entrant's own face and strokes the entrant's own nose. About fifty percent of entrants to the illusion will feel their own nose has grown longer, has even, in fact, grown incredibly long.

In describing the length of your nose, you will be tempted to exaggerate. The experience will be so new, and your listener so difficult to impress, that you will say your nose is ten feet long. Or you will say your nose is long enough to puncture the head of the person in front of you. You will avoid looking at your watch, for fear you strike your nose on your arm. You won't want to look at the floor, won't turn your head suddenly to either side, and you will walk with your left arm and your right arm thrust out beside you as though you walked on a wire.

NARCISSUSOLOGIST

The very tall
Looked down on the sky
On rain noticed mainly
By she who suggested it

What color the lenses
Dropped from the panorama
Was all by herself reinstalled

She'll get you amazing results
Her skull goes up forever
And it is white
And her whole skull
Is the first white

"I go about with you
Who nod and beckon
When I am talking
Though what you hear
Not I can say"

Leaf sheaths
Keep these ideas
Out of his hair
Just to show them
All the way in

"When I listen to
A local noise
Drowning you out
I ventriloquize
So as to keep

The uniqueness of
Our own love stressed"

Narcissus, bent on earth
Then disappeared in a coma
Without the city by a well of water
At the time that women need to draw water

action will furnish the passage
that the will to be right conceals, or you are not right,
        though you admire right, as exerted, thought-haunted,
picked up and put down
like some beast of the field all foully done

        when, therefore, afraid
        to reveal the whole operation, to pronounce it an affair
that could not quite have lasted
        through two thousand and twelve, in the season
hovering over her he felt: it's frankly possible
        she's too aware
of what she might be thinking:
        not she as a private individual
but as an army with no particular
        priority of operations: you all
might shoot her hand off
        though she'd have already
lodged a shell in your head

AN EARLY CALLER

Sometimes strip mining feels loveable

     the bowl of nosegays, replenishable flint

your chances for success

     about as small as sweeping up after

And characters lamented out of view

     prominent for their aura

of inevitability

     also the spirit

of going back to face a hunch—

     Perhaps without squinting

pruning or liking

     the real is trying out nothing

and throwing it back

     Sea changes

are the charms on the face of it:

     by their logic

what was seen in the distance

lives forever

articulated to a question mark

    expanded by, I don't know, pulling…

Bickering beneath a mass of quilts

    the keenest

do not have to reflect together

    as utterly mixed-in as they are

it is just the swindle

    you are tying to your own

capacity for memorization

    and that half-example

of a gray speedboat

    making all old turns

spreading over the bay

    like her finger through the window

wronger

    aiming to grow like herds

APTECON

Useless to trouble orioles
their long golden bores
staged in pouts to persevere
through a load of singsong, most severe…

Even the dump
hates to accept these things
Not by the hour, the day
eyes the second hand hacking its way
through sounded air

A bunch of strangers
live in the apartment now
loose ones
freed in advance
from the little fixes friends must make

If these're the new habits let them split
like hands on the arms of a chair
making room
to grow familiar, letting the head
fall forward in drowsiness
as leaves, blossoms, etc.
bend inward and sway

YOUNG NOHEJL AT NAPLES

How can property matter if I
am not in the image of myself
early and without relief
pulled out the door by winds
whose hollows support the sounds of cans
struck by falling water. The night is back
with an elder blue. At the risk of reappraisal
I am fencing off the stars, for though the name
suggests a starling, it is used by any bird, as love
is never honest or ambitious as grasped by lovers
settled down for battles. Loops of seagulls
perform their noises, lulled to the rigidity
of a mournful cop. Forever the cost of being human
will be an affront to the means of being better
as mysteriously as I repel you
and am relieved.

PLEASUROLOGIST

What are the handles on the tan can?
What are the wires?
You or I didn't have a good time
Despite the pleasure we found—we found pleasure

Rather cautious, found caution
A lie: now can barely find
Our own reflected light
Hear nothing but a plow going by. If we

're sad about speaking let's punch
Hit kick and gouge: pleasure has certain advantages
Has advantages you'll learn this in time
It's ruined when you ruin it or else
It's ruined when you ruin it yourself

The Saw That Talked

1—

Now we know Aldrin
punched a man in the jaw
for suggesting he faked the moon landing—
          an astronaut's hand

                    fell on the part of the plot
that sticks onto a smaller sub-plot
                        snapping first forward
then back, then in one diagonal, then

        in reverse along the other
both for rhythm | • | • / • \ •
and as a check against mistakes
        since if the artist

                  fails to find subject matter
or a method of working, then nothing works: your foot slips, you go down
through the soft floor
to the breakable ceiling, another floor, another ceiling

the girders stacked
since when you leapt at beauty
        then scaled it down
              to something someone

             had remarked on before
             or when you *had* that beauty
             the escaped kind
             or saw it

             or considered it, you were lost
        no hand on the jaw

could wrest you from the chase
across dirt, over ground

through odd towns
where you find the odd skies
you find if you haven't
seen many skies

2—(MAN MEANING ME)

Hunter
of heavenly bodies
emptied the bottle, dropped it into a bin for towels
left through double doors lettered Womens

"you make a chop
it turns cold you

boil a liver it
leaves you leftovers forever"

A real fable
like Bill Guard
head of Caruso's press department
charged with scoffing at rumors
of alcohol-related
vocal rest

Sooner or later Bill Guard
dug a pit in his path
and fell into it himself

Heed what narrows around you!
The shape you take in the narrows

3—(HE WARNED THE TUGS AWAY)

"You made a face," said the cop
  because he has given up
  on inference
  not tickets, tests
  of how hard you'll clutch
  and what

Tug after tug
  steamed around the ship
  looked it over
  and steamed away again

Love owed anything
  says this
  goes with that, now put
  this next to that and see if an
  arm gets out. Gets the word out. Also shoves
  a word back in

4—(LIFTING VEILS)

The cold gray rains of May
  tell half the story

I don't know who they are or what they're doing
  but I study them
  You can do
  what you need to do
  she said
  closing the phone
  closing the window

slammed shut as a speaker
by the foot of a man

amplified the beat
pattern he would need
to reach the final rhyme

5—

The worst you ever
thought was you were
controlling yourself with controls
you can wear out

You saw people travel
to visit their native lands
or those of their
parents; some even took

steps to be buried
in their native soil
or use its spices
to lend ethnic quality

to dishes of potatoes,
rice, or noodles. The
noodles themselves, where noodles
had selves, represented love

of nature, love of
anything confused: nature of
love, nature of anything
parasitic: not just one

not another then suddenly
two, but not a
second, not anything like
a next, but part

two: shelf lined with
paper, white with small
blue stars, gold with
white sea anemones: I

Don't know what it
is that Entered this
House and brought The
interference:—It was only

when game shows masked
gaps in status among
participants by using first
names and warm superficial

familiarity that we could
feel acutely the benefits
of status and produce
rules trim enough to

stay evaluation. Who is
they? They are the
same they always are
they are your others

that you love but
wonder about via hate
like different wings joined
at the same bird

6—(THE TRUSTY TOOL)

I'll let go
of the branch I was holding
to keep us stopped

Value's not produced
by hard work but by
emotional arc—you're lulled
into a dream
head against the wing
then forced awake
for survival—
what sleep
is better
than success?

If not
success
then proximity
to someone or something
successful: if not that

then a turning or clear
departure: otherwise
foolishness
to sit down
in the middle of the strip
for fear of falling
in the attempt across

7—(THE TALKATIVE SAW)

You will have to
keep looking at it
as long as you
are alive, refracting it

through info that initially
surprised you that later
you say you are
surprised you had any

surprise about—Length tolerates
need so entirely that
when you get to
the self-portrait it can

only express stupefaction at
even being there—When
you say "we don't
know what it ate

because while it ate
its snout was too
far down to see"
your friends cover you

with bodies of similar
thoughts and take yours
up to incorporate where
it fits—Just as

in the full-length closet
mirror you prove something

hinted at by a
shaving mirror mounted above

the sink—More of
each of you arrives
by train: the large
trunks held together by

ropes contain your belongings
so far—though TRULY
these objects will change
as they are discarded

8—

All this litter
a mistake: unopened cans of balls
furniture legs, coal cloth, row holders, cord
knotted to secure
something it
could or couldn't hold

In 1968 there were 3,289 pieces of litter
for each mile of United States highway
Hyphens got
bigger in litter: half-eaten, rain-soaked
sun-bleached, sand-covered, rust-crusted, shit-soiled, pee-filled
tire-crushed, tire-pounded, foot-crushed

Our reports begin
And I woke up
and I didn't know
where I was
Next is: I could see a hand
on my ankle

9—(THE LODGER)

For a year we took in a lodger—
from the divan he strolled to the tavern
and had his chops
and we followed to the tavern and had our chops

And when he was done he returned to his lodging
and when we were done we returned to ours

Then the lighthouse at the extremity
of a raised right arm
occulted: lights of ships at sea
passed in procession—some were red, some green or white
killed by a wind that came up quick
but was not cold, and foolish though we felt, we went, slowly, into obscurity
until a policeman's pager
illuminated the room: having dusted the brass
he left the detectives
who commenced resenting the intrusion
while at the bottom of a staircase a door, which he opened with a key
revealed a corridor, which he traversed, then started back, took a false step
and fell to the floor

And when he was done he returned to his lodging
and when we were done we returned to ours

10—(ACCUMULATED DELAY)

In a route, it happens, or you hear about it
At the hair place. One minute of overage
At the end of every interval
And the clock
Runs slow

Pie man / waffle woman
Asleep on a burned-out bed
Call him in the morning he'll
Play and please you in the evening

For dark was the night
Dark was always the night
And the night was light
Framed poor

11—(BALLING IT UP)

Patio access
Again restricted
Elevator access
Next

Just stay out
And never go in
Put your feet
Wholly away

YES this way the work
Of human hands is repealed
Like the work of the bouncer
Who is in it to end it

We have no fear
While we can see the sun
(It was subtle; now it's large)
You are clearly
In its query

And when results come
You'll share
Them just the way
You learned to

12—

Half a tube like a U
at the room's corner is cut
to half a tube like a C
where the cord in the tube
went cold

A night of total calm

From the neighbor a story
about a mind abandoned
to roam elsewhere, anywhere
but the neighbor's story

*Today started with me
getting woken up*

*Someone was telling me
breakfast was ready. I went out to see
if it was really ready
It was not*

Leftover in your heart
toy-like feelings
fall out as a sequence
on the scrolling LED

How I can frame it aw I don't know
cut-throat

Not that I feel that way
but that it appeals to me
to what
to feel that way

The Tax

It was anxiety that led me to love—an unsituatedness
That made me fear rest
And hate sleep—now I sleep
That I take no final faith
In what I gathered: the ideas I had
And set about testing
Like who can pull
Another up, a complexion like
A boiled root, suggestions you found
In other people's mouths
Or thought up yourself
Then fought for and stored, counting out an allotment
High enough to seem gracious, low enough to save

The sun rose or the sun sank behind a bank
Of broken clouds. If waiting is patience
Waiting to be recognized, then destiny
Is a little sarcastic, which is how I described
Blake's *Tyger, Tyger* poem in 10th grade English
For which the teacher
Mocked me—it turns out
Blake meant it, was sincere about it, and no one suggested
SARCASTIC was just one of very few words I had, like, in my vocabulary
Like people have the word DRY for wine
Because it sounds sophisticated and gives you a chance
To tell your server what you like
And you can buy a wine card
With a list of words
Like OAKY or BROAD
So you can be
Even more sophisticated
About what you'll tolerate
In this life. What did I mean? SARDONIC? AGHAST? Or just
Blake was smarter than our class
So he had a right

Not to be direct—like
A poet is a clown
In a good way
The purpose
Is to entertain people
You can be more smart than funny
Perhaps not even
Funny at all

And if something is to be a commodity and a currency
At once, like gold, or a feeling, then it's got to be subject to laws
Affecting both, though I can say
It being one
Unfits it for being the other: love
Is a feeling and I LOVE YOU
Its expression, but I LOVE YOU
Begets an I LOVE YOU back, or it falters
As it its harbor
Fails to find. I LOVE YOU
Is what I trade you, a thing
And I try not
To drive down the value
Of a thing. Implicit love
Can be described
But not remanded
And if ever it multiplied
To take away
That currency power
Its allegiance to barter
Well then I would just be cheated

She said I never wear panties
Even when I'm playing a cold city
As though panties
Were for warmth

What she's doing
Is a trick if you
Think about it
The knack
Of coupling sensations
That pass from top to bottom
Like the best sensation
May be one you know you can remove, an unpleasant
Film on your fingers
After you use them
To mix some meal: you know you can
Wash, you know you're just tolerating
Something that can be relieved—and maybe that's
The notch that unbelief
Yields in the structure's foundation: they *are* structures
These arrangements: living together
Sleeping alongside, staying awake while the other one sleeps. You have
To care! Be the sun
Shining through a watery cloud, or the cloud
Creased to a white veil
Since where you believe you have power you don't
And where you do you refuse to wield it

But I don't know should people
Who show a little doubt
In what they do
Always lose? Who wants to be
Reassuring all the time it'd be
Like a job. And it's so
Public too it's not
Like we won't ever have much
To go on about
That's the best part
About being gone
Rosy hill, buck-colored dale, heaving

Old enemies over: nothing
Owned, just borrowed
One soul from another in the throes
Golden throes
Ones meant to make the most
Of an exchange
Picked out of the air, like a flower
Cut out from some pot, just to let
This impression fall away
Without considering
What you are letting it fall away from

Some of these poems first appeared in the following publications: *6x6, Aphros, Big Bell, Boston Review, Chicago Review, DC Poetry, Fence, Highway Robbery, No: A Journal of the Arts, The Poetry Project Newsletter, The Poker, Realpoetik, Zoland Poetry,* and in the chapbooks *The Garden of Eden a College* (A Rest Press) and *The Saw That Talked* (Minutes Books).

This book was published in an edition of 1,000 copies. It was printed and bound by McNaughton & Gunn using covers printed at Printing Gallery and at the Ugly Duckling Presse workshop. The text was typeset in Caslon.

Ugly Duckling Presse is a nonprofit publishing collective devoted to the dissemination of new works of poetry and translation, lost works, theatrical and hybrid texts, books by artists, and compelling investigative works regardless of genre.

www.uglyducklingpresse.org